THELMA BESS

SPIRITUAL

MATURITY

TRANSFORMATION

RENEWING THE MIND

RELENTLESS
PUBLISHING

Spiritual Maturity Transformation : Renewing The Mind
Copyright © 2020 by Thelma Bess.

Published by:
Relentless Publishing House
www.relentlesspublishing.com

RELENTLESS
PUBLISHING

ISBN: 9781948829359

Table of Contents

Spiritual

Maturity

Transformation

"Spiritual maturity is neither instant nor automatic; it is gradual, progressive development that will take the rest of your life."

-Rick Warren

INTRODUCTION

Theme Scripture:

Romans 12:2
And be not conformed to this world: but be ye transformed by the renewing of your mind, that ye may prove what is that good, and acceptable, and perfect, will of God. (KJV)

Spiritual is related to godly values. Maturity means growth or development. When you merge Spiritual Maturity together it defines a process that develops, shape, mold that builds spiritual maturity or spiritual values. This book will discuss ways to experience a closer relationship with God. Spiritual Maturity is an act or process that transforms the new man's character to be more like Christ. Character is who we are and our reputation is who people think we are. Character comes from what you say and do. Why is Spiritual Maturity necessary? We must first know the purpose before we can commit to change.

Gen 2:7 "And the LORD God formed man of the dust of the ground, and breathed into his nostrils the breath of life; and man became a living soul." Adam and Eve had a personal relationship with God. God visited them each day and they were in fellowship with God. The first man and woman sinned in the garden of Eden and was driven out of the garden. Sin will always drive you away from God. We are born in sin and separated from God. Because of our sinful nature, we must grow or develop our new man after we accept Jesus Christ as our Lord and Saviour. We must allow the Holy Spirit to work in our life.

The Holy Spirit indwells us; but it's dormant (inactive). Acts 2:2 "And suddenly there came a sound from heaven as of a rushing mighty wind, and it filled all the house where they were sitting." And it fell upon everyone in the house. When we accept Jesus, we become a new creature.

Spiritual maturity is a continuous process. "Not that I have already obtained all this, or have already been made perfect, but I press on to take hold of that for which Christ Jesus took hold of me. Brothers, I do not consider myself yet to have taken hold of it. But one thing I do: Forgetting what is behind and straining toward what is ahead, I press on toward the goal to win the prize for which God has called me heavenward in Christ Jesus" (Philippians 3:12-14 NIV). Paul had not arrived, but he continually pressed toward the prize. Paul knew spiritual maturity was necessary for the new man to be in fellowship with God.

Your beliefs become your thoughts,

Your thoughts become your words,

Your words become your actions,

Your actions become your habits,

Your habits become your values,

Your values become your destiny.

-Gandhi

2Cor 5:17 "Therefore if any man be in Christ, he is a new creature: old things are passed away; behold, all things are become new." We become a new man; what happens to the old man. The old man doesn't move out. We have to evict the old man, put him out. How do you evict the old man? The new man must renew the mind with renewed knowledge. The new man must develop a closer relationship with God that focus more on God and less on self.

What are some character traits of the old man that causes the new man to evict him?

_____

_____

_____

_____

_____

_____

_____

_____

_____

_____

_____

_____

_____

LESSON ONE:

Spiritual Maturity Evaluation

Lesson Scripture: 1 Peter 2:2

As newborn babies, desire the sincere milk of the word, that ye may grow thereby

God's will for every person is to experience growth and maturity as a Christian. Maturity is not based on age, appearance, achievements or academics. Maturity is determined by our attitude. It is your attitude that impacts your character. Attitude is the way you think and act and character is who you are. We must commit to spiritual maturity, so we can fulfill Christ's command that we love our neighbor as ourselves. "**As newborn babies, desire the sincere milk of the word, that ye may grow thereby**: (1 Peter 2:2)

Physical and Spiritual maturity begins with birth. Physical maturity begins with the baby parents and spiritual maturity begins with you. A baby is harmless and helpless. A baby depends on the parents or caregivers. A baby conception to birth is approximately 9 months and society says the age of maturity is 21 years old. Spiritual Maturity starts immediately after we accept Jesus as our Lord and Saviour. A newborn baby eats about 8 times a day and as they grow older the feeding is reduce; because the baby is able digest more milk at a feeding. Spiritual Maturity requires a desire for the sincere milk of the word. We should start reading God's word and we should increase our time reading God's Word as we mature in Christ. Christian Education, Sunday School, Bible Study, and seminar classes provides the milk; but everyone will not receive this milk. We set goals for everything else. Why shouldn't we set goals for spiritual maturity?

1. How do you handle problems?   James 1:2, 12

Verse 2: My brethren, count it all joy when ye fall into divers temptations

Verse 12: Blessed is the man that endureth temptation: for when he is tried, he shall receive the crown of life, which the Lord hath promised to them that love him.

Can we show kindness when others are treating you wrong? We should see problems as opportunity to grow. Don't pretend it doesn't hurt; it's an opportunity for joy. Tough times can teach us to persevere.

_____

_____

2. How do you treat others?   Col. 3:12-14

Verse 12:   Put on therefore, as the elect of God, holy and beloved, bowels of mercies, kindness, humbleness of mind, meekness, longsuffering;

Verse 13:   Forbearing one another, and forgiving one another, if any man have a quarrel against any: even as Christ forgave you, so also do ye

Verse 14:   And above all these things put on charity, which is the bond of perfectness.

Do you make allowances? Do you have a forgiving attitude? Does love guide you?

_____

_____

3. Do you control what you say?   James 3:2, 5; Eph. 4:29

James 3:2, 5
Verse 2: For in many things we offend all. If any man offend not in word, the same is a perfect man, and able also to bridle the whole body.

Verse 5: Even so the tongue is a little member, and boasteth great things. Behold, how great a matter a little fire kindleth!

Ephesians 4:29
Let no corrupt communication proceed out of your mouth, but that which is good to the use of edifying, that it may minister grace unto the hearers.

4. What you say and don't say is important. Let everything you say be good and helpful.

_____

_____

5. What affect do you have on others, positive or negative (Instigator)? Rom 12:18

Verse 18: If it be possible, as much as lieth in you, live peaceably with all men.

_____

_____

6. How much do you depend on God?   Is God your last result? Prov 3:5

Verse 5: Trust in the LORD with all thine heart; and lean not unto thine own understanding

_____

_____

Notes

_____

_____

_____

_____

_____

_____

_____

_____

_____

_____

_____

Exercise: Spiritual Goals Planner

List Spiritual Goals you would like to implement in your life:

_____

_____

_____

List actions you will take to implement the spiritual goals:

_____

_____

_____

List scriptures that will encourage you to meet your spiritual goals:

_____

_____

_____

Spiritual Goals Examples

My action plan:

- Read the word daily
- Set devotional time to meditate on God's word
- Participate in a bible study or Sunday school
- Write a scripture in your journal to memorize the word

Purchase a notebook to start a journal for your Spiritual goals!

LESSON TWO:

Transformation

Lesson Scripture: Romans 12:2

"And be not conformed to this world: but be ye transformed by the renewing of your mind, that ye may prove what is that good, and acceptable, and perfect, will of God."

The transformation process starts by reading God's Word and praying without ceasing. When we change the way we think, then we will know what God wants and requires for us.

1. **What is conformed**? Being fashioned, modeling or behavior, world standard, reflecting or looking like the world.

We should avoid acting like the world. Our new identity should be transformed by the renewing of the mind. *Old things are passed away, behold all things become new.* (2 Cor 5:17) Renewing of the mind is the key to transformation. The Holy Spirit gives us a new identity. We are not reformed; we are re-created (**new creature**). Reform is to improve; we don't want to improve the old man, he has to go (evicted). When we accept Christ, we begin a new life with a new Master. Before we accepted Christ, Satan was our master. A lot of Christians are participating in Identity Theft. How? Conforming to the world, stealing Satan's identity. We must renew our minds, change the way we think and change our identity by renewing the mind. Our name stays the same our character changes.

2. **What is Transformation?** Transformed is complete or total change from the inside out. A change must take place for a transformation. If you take a person and clean them up and they don't change the way they think (mind), they will remain the same.

Butterfly: A butterfly goes through a transformation process. It starts out as a caterpillar; it crawls and is not pretty like a butterfly. A butterfly flies and is beautiful. In order for a butterfly to transform from a caterpillar, the caterpillar must die. It falls apart. We must go through a transformation, but we try to cling to what we know, our old habits and will not surrender to God. Have your life been upside down or you felt like everything was falling apart. You may be going through a transformation, don't resist.

3. **Why does our mind need to be Renewed?** The mind directs the actions of the body. 2 Cor 4:16 "*For which cause we faint not; but though our outward man perish, yet the inward man is renewed day by day.*" The mind is the focus point of our perception, morals, values, and behavior. Unlike a computer, we can't delete the information, once stored in our mind; it's there forever. The information is archived. A related word or statement will recall the memory. We have to allow God to renew, re-educate and re-direct our mind.

4. **What is proving and what do we need to prove?** Prove is Testing and we must test our mind. Our mind is like a computer, sometime we need to run an Anti-Virus Program. We must test ideas, actions, activities, doctrine, motives, agenda, our friends, our thoughts, etc. to make sure they are in the Will of God. Good means good for us, good in us, and acceptable to God.

5. **What is renewed knowledge?** We must realize who we were in God's sight before He saved us. We were in a fallen state, a part of Satan's world, rebellious, separated from God. When we came to Christ, we were identified with Him. We put off the old identity and we are no longer who we once were. We are a new creature.

_____

_____

_____

_____

_____

_____

If you keep yourself pure, you will be a special utensil for honorable use. Your life will be clean, and you will be ready for the Master to use you for every good work.

2 Timothy 2:21

LESSON THREE:

Knowledge is Power (God's Word)

"Knowledge is not what you can, but what you cannot forget." ~ Unknown

Lesson Scripture: 2 Timothy 2:15

"Study to shew thyself approved unto God, a workman that needeth not to be ashamed, rightly dividing the word of truth."

We must have a strong desire for God's Word which is called the sincere milk of the word. When we read God's Word, it should be to transform and not inform. In order to have a personal relationship with God, we must **commit time** to reading God's Word. We make time for everything, but God. Psalms 119:105 *"Thy word is a lamp unto my feet, and a light unto my path."* The Word of God is like a torch, it shows us the way, prevents us from stumbling over obstacles or falling down. Light unto my path, a light shines on the road; so you can see the path. A Christian should make the Word of God their guide.

List things we can purge after reading God's Word

_____

_____

_____

Consider purging some of the items listed in the table below.

Old Attitudes	Envy	Double Minded
Lying Tongue	Lust	Anger
Gossip	Quarreling	Habits

When we read the Word of God, we should let the Word interrupt, rearrange, and redirect. Knowledge is power and reading God's Word can lead to salvation, guide our life, give wisdom, lift heavy burden, bring joy, and give peace. The Word of God is infallible. There is no error in the Word of God. All scriptures are God given. God's Word is true; but all scriptures are not truths for us to live by. Some scriptures are example of those that strayed from God or His Word.

Reading God's Word will help you understand God's requirements for our new life. When we read God's Word and apply the Word to our life, it will develop or grow our new man.

God has made us a free will people and we must choose to live by God's Word. We must be **Readers and Doers** of the **Word**.

a. How do you increase your reading time?

_____

_____

b. How do you apply God's Word to your life?

_____

_____

c. How do you memorize the Word of God? Why memorize the word?

_____

_____

We should read the Word, Hear the Word, read the Word aloud, meditate on the Word, and Obey the Word by living the Word.

Exercise on Reading God's Word:

Read 2Cor 5:17: *Therefore if any man be in Christ, he is a new creature: old things are passed away; behold, all things are become new.*

As you read 2Cor 5:17 recognize God is speaking to you. Take time to hear God. Read the scriptures and allow the words to transform you. Read the words slowly to hear the intent and message God has for you in His Word.

What was God's Message to You in 2Cor 5:17?

_____

_____

What will you purge from your life after reading 2Cor 5:17?

_____

_____

Memorize:

In the Word of God, I see the Son of God and I am transformed by the Spirit of God, so that I can live out the Will of God.

A Plan to Reads God's Word

Read through the New Testament 5 days a week, 10 minutes a day.

10 minutes a day | If you're not currently reading the Bible, start with 10 minutes a day. This reading plan will take you through the New Testament, one chapter per day.

5 days a week | It helps to schedule a time and location to spend 10 minutes a day reading God's word. Find a quiet place where you can regularly read and meditate on God's word.

Ways to dig deeper | We must meditate to allow the word to take effect in our lives. Below are ways for a detail study of God's word.

Underline or highlight key words or phrases in the Bible passage. Use a pen or highlighter to mark new discoveries from the text. Periodically review your markings to see what God is teaching you.

1. Find a reading plan for the New Testament that works with your schedule.
2. Read the passage or verses slowly and add your name in the verse to make it personaa.
3. Always note who (person), what (event), when (time frame), where (location), audience (to whom it was written). This will help you understand the purpose of the scripture.
4. God speaks to us through the scripture. We must respond. Ask yourself this question, "What will I change after reading God's word today?"

Reading God's Word

1. Pray for a hunger for God's Word.

In Psalms 119 we can see the psalmist's love and hunger for God's word. In verse 103: *"How sweet are Your words to my taste! Sweeter than honey to my mouth!"* We, too, can have this kind of joy in God's Word; we can ask God to give us a hunger and a taste for His Word.

2. Choose a set time to read.

It helps to schedule a set time for reading the Bible. Morning, during lunch or before going to bed can be a good time to read. A scheduled time helps us remember to read the Word and makes it a part of our daily routine.

3. Read consecutively.

A good way to help us regularly and consistently read the Word is to read it consecutively, chapter after chapter and book after book. This way we don't have to decide what to read each time, and as we read the Bible cover to cover we'll begin to see God at work throughout the Bible.

4. Turn your heart to the Lord before reading.

Every time we come to the Word, it's good to **turn our heart** to the Lord. Reading the Bible, we should pray a simple prayer like this:

> *"Lord, as I read your word, I turn my heart toward You. I will be open to hear what You are saying. Speak to me, wash me and allow the word to a lamp unto my feat so my path will be clear. Amen!"*

5. Pray over what you read.

Sometimes as we're reading the Bible, a certain verse stands out to us. It may comfort us, convict us, or apply exactly to our situation. We can stop and pray what we've read back to the Lord. We might thank the Lord or praise Him for certain portions, we might ask Him to show us the meaning of a certain verse, or we might just talk with Him about a verse.

Exercise: Breakthrough Movie (2019)
Based on the Impossible True Story

Play the selected clips below from the 2019 Movie **Breakthrough** and discuss the clips. Discuss each clip below and determine if it demonstrates Spiritual Maturity. If so, why; if not, why?

Introduction to the Movie Breakthrough

Tragedy strikes when Joyce Smith's adopted son, John falls through the ice on a frozen lake in Missouri. Trapped underwater for more than 15 minutes, rescuers pull John back to the surface and rush him to the nearest hospital where he is pronounced dead after 45 minutes of resuscitation efforts. His mother goes into the room and prays to God and his heart starts beating. John is airlifted to a bigger hospital where Dr. Garrett, an expert in his field doesn't think he will live through the night. (True Story)

Play the following clips and discuss Spiritual Maturity:

1. Joyce leads a woman Bible Study. (Observe Joyce's Character)

   _____

   _____

2. Emergency Room Scene after they declare him dead. (Observe Joyce's faith and prayer life)

   _____

   _____

3. Meeting with Dr. Garrett (expert in his field) at the bigger hospital. (Observe Joyce's attitude)

   _____

   _____

4. Lobby with support Groups and Friends, Joyce lose her temper. (Observe Joyce's reputation)

_____

_____

5. Joyce's Roof Top Experience. (Observe Joyce's transformation)

_____

_____

6. Community Support outside the window singing. (Observe the community's humblesness and kindess)

_____

_____

7. The Miracle – Dr. Garrett declares John a miracle. (God is Almighty, want God do it)

_____

_____

Notes:

_____

_____

_____

_____

_____

_____

_____

_____

_____

_____

_____

_____

_____

_____

_____

_____

LESSON FOUR:

In God's Presence (Prayer)

Lesson Scripture: Matthew 6:6

But thou, when thou prayest, enter into thy closet, and when thou hast shut thy door, pray to thy Father which is in secret; and thy Father which seeth in secret shall reward thee openly.

What is Prayer?

_____

_____

God desires to have an intimate relationship with each one of us. The only way to have a relationship with God is through prayer. Prayer is our only communication with God. Prayer is talking to God, meditating and allowing Him to speak to us. Sometime we hang up on God; before God can speak back to us. Prayer is a time when we enter the presence of God. Prayer is a privilege. *"Pray without ceasing."* (1Th 5:17) As believers, we should recognize our absolute dependency on God.

A strong prayer life means you have a strong signal with God. There are a lot of Christians who have lost their connection with God. When this happen your prayer life is no longer effective. We can't afford to be in a dead zone with our prayer life or out of fellowship with God. A Christian must stay connected to God at all time.

Prayer is the first step in developing our new man. Matthew 26:41 "*Watch and pray, that ye enter not into temptation: the spirit indeed is willing, but the flesh is weak.*" We must prepare our hearts for prayer. Pray and ask God to give us the strength through His Holy Spirit to understand changes needed in our life. "*Commit thy way unto the LORD; trust also in him; and he shall bring it to pass.*" (Psalms 37:5)

When we pray publicly our prayers should be for the body and not for ourselves. How often should we pray? Are you a doubter? Doubt makes us question God's Word and his goodness. Doubt makes you look at your problems rather than God. Doubt makes you feel like a failure. Doubt keeps you from trying. Doubt will delay your blessings. There are two groups of Prayers (Responding and Asking).

A. Responding Prayers

Responding Prayers respond to God as a person. Responding Prayers include **confession, praise, worship, and thanksgiving**. Confession acknowledges sin. Praise is adoration focus on God and responding to God's character or attributes. Worship is responding to God's glory. Worship is adoring, loving and honoring God. Thanksgiving is an attitude of gratitude. When God reveals Himself by blessings you, Giving thanks to Him is a natural response.

B. Asking Prayers

The Bible teaches two types of Asking Prayers, Petition and Intercession. God answers Asking Prayers to accomplish His Will. Asking Prayers should be led by the Holy Spirit. Petition is asking for yourself, your family, your church, or others. Intercession is petitioning on the behalf of someone else.

C. Hindered Prayers (Daniel 10:13)

Allow your mind to think on this thought, what if God has already answered your prayer and your answer was hindered by Satan. God answered Daniel's prayer the moment He received it; but Satan hindered it. Daniel was steadfast and unmovable in prayer and continued to pray expecting God to answer His prayer. Sometimes we hang up before God answer reaches us.

Then there are times we expect God to answer us in a certain way or through a certain person and we miss our blessing. God will use the least expected person to answer our prayer. There are times when God says no to our prayers and it is in those times we must remain faithful. When God says no to us it is for a reason.

A no from God is a blessing. No can mean a better quality of life for us. How many here today have experienced when God has said, "No?" You didn't understand the no, but later on or years later a praise came in your heart and you thanked God for the no. God always knows what is best for you. We don't know God's thoughts and His ways are not our ways. His timing is not our timing. One thing we can be assured of is God is always on time.

The Model Prayer (Matthew 6:9-13)

There are six Petitions in the Model Prayer; 3 petitions toward God and 3 petitions toward man.

Our Father who art in Heaven:

It shows a personal relationship, we have accepted Him as our Father which means we are His child.

1st Petition: Hallow Be Thy Name (His Name)

Hallow means Holy, we should give Him honor and respect. God's name represent His authority, reputation, and character (omnipresence, omniscient, omnipotent.) Our motive should be to bring honor and glory not shame.

2nd Petition: Thy Kingdom Come (His Reign)

Jesus is King and a King must Reign. We must submit to his reign in our life. We are expecting Christ's second coming where we will reign with Him.

3rd Petition: Thy Will Be Done (His Will)

We must surrender our all to God. We must submit to God's rule in our life and His will for our life.

4th Petition: Give Us This Day our Daily Bread (Daily Needs)

We are trusting God for our provision. A man must work to eat. God is our provider, everything belongs to God. The air that we breathe belongs to God, the next breath we take.

5th Petition: Forgive Us Our Debts (Our Sins)

Sin is a debt that must be released. Christ released us from the penalty of sin before we were born. We should always confess our sin to God and should have a forgiving attitude. No one owes us an apology.

6th Petition: Deliver Us From Evil Lead (Our Temptation)

God doesn't tempt anyone (James 1:13). We should be praying for the Spirit to help us recognize temptation and give us strength to overcome it. The model prayer begins with God and ends with God. For thine is the Kingdom, and the power, and the glory. Amen. He is worthy to be Praised. Our motives for praying must be pure.

There are eight main things that have to happen in prayer (2Chronicles 7:14). God's people need to do five of those things and because of our limitations God has do the other three things.

The eight steps found in 2 Chronicles 7:14: *If my people, which are called by my name, shall humble themselves, and pray, and seek my face, and turn from their wicked ways; then will I hear from heaven, and will forgive their sin, and will heal their land.*

1. Know that we are God's people
2. Humble ourselves
3. Pray with Power
4. Seek God
5. Turn from our wicked ways (repent)

Then God will...

6. Hear every prayer
7. Forgive our sins
8. Heal our land

When we pray as a group; we should pray in Unity. **Unity is the state of being united into a whole or one purpose and one goal**.

Write down a prayer request that is weighing on your heart.

_____

_____

_____

_____

_____

_____

_____

Reference: In God's Presence by Claud V. King and T.W. Hunt.

Exercise

Sometimes our actions represent who we are spiritually more than our words. Ask yourself the following questions:

1. **Do you seek God and have a desire for a closer relationship?**

   _____

   _____

2. **How much time do you spend reading God's Word?**

   _____

   _____

3. **Do you apply the Word of God to your life after hearing it?**

   _____

   _____

4. **When God reveals sin in your life, do you confess and repent?**

   _____

   _____

Notes:

_____

_____

_____

_____

_____

The Word Hand illustration is an easy- to-remember tool highlighting five methods of learning from the Bible.

Use it for your own spiritual growth and share it with someone else.

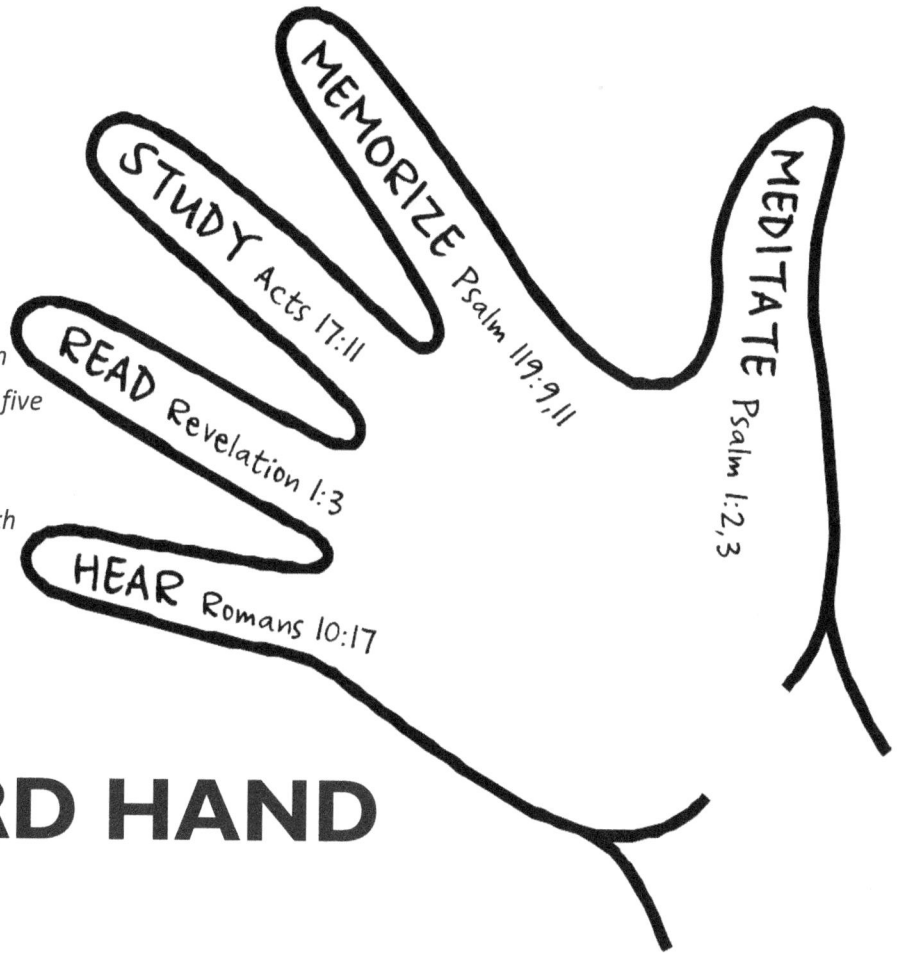

STUDY Acts 17:11

MEMORIZE Psalm 119:9,11

READ Revelation 1:3

MEDITATE Psalm 1:2,3

HEAR Romans 10:17

THE WORD HAND

1 **HEARING** the Word from pastors and teachers provides fresh insight into the Scriptures. The weakest finger—the pinkie— represents hearing, because we retain only 5 percent of what we hear. *Romans 10:17*

2 **READING** gives us an overview of the Bible and is the foundation of a daily quiet time.
This is represented by the ring finger. We generally retain 15 percent of what we read. Revelation 1:3

3 **STUDYING** the Scriptures deepens our convictions. It requires greater time and effort but results in increased Bible knowledge. Most people retain 35 percent of what they study. This is represented by the middle finger. *Acts 17:11*

4 **MEMORIZING** God's Word *prepare* us to overcome temptations and to have verses memorized to minister to others. The index finger, our strongest finger, represents memorization. We remember 100 percent of what we memorize, if we consistently review it. *Psalm 119:9–11*

5 **MEDITATION** is the inward process that supports each of the other four methods of Scripture intake. This is why meditation is assigned to the thumb. Only the thumb can touch all the other four fingers. By meditating on God's Word as we hear, read, study, and memorize, we discover its transforming power at work in us. *Psalm 1:2-3*

Prayer Journal

Date:_____

I prayed to God for the following blessings:

_____

_____

_____

_____

_____

On _____ God answered my prayers in the following ways:

_____

_____

_____

_____

I shared my testimony with the following people:

_____

_____

_____

_____

LESSON FIVE:

Forgiveness (Letting It Go!)

Reference: Free to Forgive: Jeff Jeffress

Lesson Scripture: Ephesians 4:32

And be ye kind one to another, tenderhearted, forgiving one another, even as God for Christ's sake hath forgiven you.

Forgiveness is to pardon, or release from payment. Forgiveness is a debt that must be released. Eph 4:32 states, "*And be ye kind one to another, tenderhearted, forgiving one another, even as God for Christ's sake hath forgiven you.*" We must follow Christ's method in forgiveness. Remember, no one owes you an apology. If they give you an apology Hallelujah, if they don't Hallelujah any how.   Romans 5:8 states, "*But God commendeth his love toward us, in that, while we were yet sinners, Christ died for us.*" We deserved to go to hell; but God offered us a pardon and we must pardon others. We must learn to forgive others just as Christ has forgiven us. **Don't negotiate**. We must release them and we shouldn't require anything in return. (Luke 7:41-42) The lender was the innocent party; but he forgave them. Someone will always have to pay; because the offense causes an obligation.   When we forgive we must recognize a wrong has occurred and the wrong has created an obligation of repayment; then we should choose to release the offender from the obligation and to accept the wrong as an experience on this Christian Journey. Some people are afraid to forgive; because they feel it will give the offender power or permission to hurt them again. Peter asks Jesus how many times shall I forgive my brother when he sins against me? Up to seven times, Jesus responded "*seventy times seven*" (Matt 18:21-22). Forgiveness starts in the heart and ends with an apology to stay in fellowship with the offender. We must pray and ask God to guide us when it's the proper time to approach the person. It may be too soon! **Test the water**.

We must learn to focus on how the other person feels and try to understand their point of view without resentment. Always remember, God sees all things and hears everything; He hears when we say ugly things to our brothers and sisters in Christ. When we say ugly things to people; we are saying them to God too. 1 Cor 3:16: *Know ye not that ye are the temple of God, and that the Spirit of God dwelleth in you.* Forgiveness guards our heart from bitterness (resentment, animosity, and hostility). When we truly forgive a person, we cast the disagreements into the sea of forgiveness.

There is no such thing as forgive and forget. We can't erase our memory. When Satan brings the past hurt to our memory (our computer or mind calls it up) that is why it is important to suppress it right way.

We must rebuke the thought in the name of Jesus and pray to God for strength to resist the thought. We can't resist it on our own. After receiving forgiveness from God, we should pass it along to others. If you are having a problem forgiving, seek a closer walk with God. 1 John 4:20 states, "*If a man say, I love God, and hateth his brother, he is a liar: for he that loveth not his brother whom he hath seen, how can he love God whom he hath not seen?*" So, Let It Go! Free to Forgive, Robert Jeffress book.

Root of Bitterness (Heart Condition)

Forgiveness is a condition of the heart. When we forgive; we promise never to raise the matter as an issue for discussion with that person. (Romans 12:21 "Don't let evil get the best of you, get the best of evil by doing good.") When we forgive; we promise never to bring up the matter with others. When we forgive; we promise not to think on the offense in our mind. Why? It will come back to your remembrance; but you shouldn't dwell on it. Satan is ready, willing, and able to cause confusion. Saul attack on David was a Root of Bitterness. Envy and Jealousy is root of bitterness.

There are three reasons to forgive.

1. Forgive for your own good

As long as you refuse to let go of hurt, you've tied the other person to you. One person put it this way: "We're giving that person free rent inside our heads." Consider the cost of not forgiving: the energy and emotion you give to the hurt throughout the day or the sleep you may lose. This could go on for years. Inner peace is impossible, when you don't forgive. When bitterness festers, the infection grows and damages our relationships with others and God. Forgiveness offers us freedom to move on, so we can continue living.

2. Forgive because it pleases God

Instead of asking, "Why should I forgive? It's their fault not mine," we must realize forgiveness frees us from pain. Jesus taught us to pray, *"If you forgive those who sin against you, your heavenly Father will forgive you. But if you refuse to forgive others, your Father will not forgive your sins.* (Matthew 6:14-15 NLT).

3. Forgive because you have experienced God's grace for your sins

We have received God's grace - forgiveness - which we don't deserve. No matter what we done, God's grace wipes away every wrongdoing. When we realize we don't deserve God's forgiveness, we will be ready to release others.

List someone you need to forgive.

_____

_____

It is possible for you to forgive them right now. If you want to stay in fellowship with them; then you will go to them personally and make amends, even if it's not your fault.

"Be ye angry, and sin not: let not the sun go down upon your wrath" Eph 4:26

Notes

_____

_____

_____

_____

_____

_____

_____

_____

_____

_____

_____

_____

_____

Letting It Go

The same evil that motivated our offender to hurt us reside in us and we should pray God doesn't allow it to come out. The Blame Game – It's easier to blame than to forgive. Sometimes: Why did God allow this hurt in my life?

Gen 3: Adam and Evil sinned; but God didn't require anything. He went looking for them and He prepared the covering before they acknowledge the need for the covering. Repentance and remorse are necessary to receive forgiveness, but not required to grant forgiveness. Grace is giving someone something good that they don't deserve. Christ died for us; before we were ever born.

Case Against Forgiveness (Reasons Not to Forgive)

1. What I did doesn't matter and it didn't hurt me
2. I'm letting them off the hook
3. Forgiveness puts pressure on me
4. Forgiveness is not fair

Releasing the Person who has offended you (Debtor-Matthew 18:21-35)

5. Lender had a legal right (innocent)
6. The borrowers had legal obligation to pay (guilty)
7. The borrower didn't have the money to repay
8. Someone always has to pay
9. Forgiveness is the only way to settle the debt
10. Forgiveness frees us to go on with our life

Forgiveness

Agree or Disagree:
- Forgiving a person without an apology allow them to hurt you again

Agree or Disagree
- Forgiving a person without an apology goes against the Bible

Forgiveness: Letting It Go!

1. **List reasons it's hard to forgive at times:**

   _____

   _____

   _____

2. **List past hurts you need to release:**

   _____

   _____

   _____

3. **List people you need to forgive:**

   _____

   _____

   _____

E – Easy   N – Not Easy   H – Hard to Do

	Can you forgive yourself?
	Can you forgive when a person has hurt you repeatedly? (over and over again)
	Can you forgive when a person spreads false rumors on you?
	Can you forgive when it really hurts?
	Can you ask others for forgiveness?
	Can you admit you have been hurt?
	Can you acknowledge the debt you are owed and release the offender of their obligation?

Y – Yes   N - No

	Are you suffering from a guilty conscience?
	Do you wish you could erase your memory or past?
	Is it easier to blame than to forgive?

LESSON SIX:

Sowing the Seeds (Fruit of the Spirit)

Lesson Scripture: Galatians 5:22-23

But the fruit of the Spirit is love, joy, peace, longsuffering, gentleness, goodness, faith, Meekness, temperance: against such there is no law.

Sow a thought, reap an action; sow an action, reap a habit; sow a habit, reap a character; sow a character, reap a destiny. Our character will determine our destiny. If we honestly admit, "I am what I am today because of the choices I made yesterday," then we say, "**I choose to change**."

To learn and not to do is really not to learn. To know and not to do is really not to know.   It is one thing to make a mistake, and another thing not to admit it. People will forgive mistakes, because mistakes are usually of the mind, mistakes of judgment. Our behavior is a function of our decisions, not our conditions. How you treat one reveals how you regard the many, because everyone is ultimately a one.

Fruit of the Spirit:
The Fruit of the Spirit is the work of the Holy Spirit in us. The Spirit produces the character traits found in Jesus. In order to grow the Fruit of the Spirit, we must love

God and give the Holy Spirit an opportunity work in our life. A complete harvest of the Fruit of the Spirit produces nine qualities. The first three qualities are Love, Joy, and

Peace and deal with the believer's heart and mind and come from our relationship with God. Love in our heart, joy in our daily life, and peace with God.

Love seeks the highest good for others. Love is a decision to be committed to the well being of others without any conditions or circumstances. Love is the foundation of all the Fruit of the Spirit and Jesus demonstrated unconditional and self sacrificing love by dying for us. (John 3:16, 13:1, 15:13)

Joy comes from our relationship with God and from knowing the penalty of sin has been removed and we have been pardon. Joy is a gladness not based on our circumstances. Joy comes from obeying God's Will. (John 17:13)

Peace is the state of assurance, lack of fear, and contentment. Peace comes from our relationship with God. We are no longer enemies of God and have been delivered from the penalty of sin. (Colossians 3:15, Philippians 4:7)

The second three qualities are Longsuffering, Gentleness, and Goodness and we use these qualities in our relationship with each other.

Longsuffering or patience means to endure or to put up with. Longsuffering gives us patience or restraint and keeps us from acting hastily in disagreement, opposition, or persecution. Patience is slow to speak and slow to anger. (Matthew 27:14, James 1:3-4, 12)

Gentleness is kindness and is shown to everyone with no respect of person. Kindness is merciful, sweet, and tender.

Goodness is to do good to others. Goodness is generous and open hearted. Goodness is the desire to be open hearted and generous to others without seeking anything in return.

The last three qualities are Faith, Meekness, and Temperance and are manifested in the believer.

Faith is trust or assurance. Faith deals with unseen realities and faith is the foundation of our hope to receive what God has promise us. Faith helps us to remain dependable, loyal, and full of trust.

Meekness is strength under control. Meekness demonstrates a humble spirit.

Temperance is moderation or self control. Temperance will control emotions, actions, and desires.

List other godly traits we can sow into our life:

_____

_____

Generosity, Integrity, Loyalty, Kindness, Hospitality, Self-control.

_____

_____

Love will enable us to appreciate our brothers and sisters in the Lord, and, of course, our family, and others around us. Love is taking the initiative to build up and meet the needs of others without expecting anything in return. (John 13:1; 15:13; 1 Corinthians 13:3)

Joy will allow us to enjoy His creation, others, and our circumstances with an expression of delight and real, authentic happiness from and with harmony with God and others. (Proverbs 15:13; John 15:11; 17:13)

Peace is surrendering and yielding to the Lord's control, for He is our ultimate peace! It is allowing tranquility to be our tone and to control our equanimity. This will be fueled by our harmonious relationship with God so we can hand over control of our heart, will, and mind to Him. Once we make real peace with God, we will be able to make and maintain peace with others. (Matthew 5:9; Colossians 3:15; Philippians 4:7)

Patience is showing tolerance and fortitude to others, and even accepting difficult situations from them and God without making demands and conditions. (Matthew 27:14; Romans 12:12; James 1:3,12)

Kindness is practicing benevolence and a loving attitude towards others. (Ephesians 4:32)

Goodness displays integrity, honesty, and compassion to others, and allows us to do the right thing. (Matthew 19:16)

Faithfulness is the "gluing" fruit that will preserve our faith and the other characters of the Spirit as well as identify God's Will so we can be dependable and trusting to God and others. (Matthew 17:19; 25:21; 1 Cor. 12:9; Hebrews 11:1; 1 Thess. 5:24)

Gentleness is the character that will show calmness, personal care, and tenderness in meeting the needs of others. (Isa. 40:11; Phil. 4: 5; 2 Timothy 2:24; 1 Thess. 2:7)

Self-Control will allow us to have discipline, and restraint with obedience to God and others. (1 Thess. 5: 22)

LESSON SEVEN:

Spiritual Gifts

Lesson Scripture: 1 Corinthians 12:7-10

But the manifestation of the Spirit is given to every man to profit withal. For to one is given by the Spirit the word of wisdom; to another the word of knowledge by the same Spirit; To another faith by the same Spirit; to another the gifts of healing by the same Spirit; To another the working of miracles; to another prophecy; to another discerning of spirits; to another divers kinds of tongues; to another the interpretation of tongues.

Spiritual Gifts are God given abilities to be used for the up building of His Kingdom. 1 Corinthians 12:7-10. Spiritual gifts qualify us to do something we couldn't normally do. Spiritual gifts are different from talents. Talents are natural and spiritual gifts are received from God. Talents can be inherited from family and used for selfish motives. Spiritual Gifts are used to serve others. 1 Peter 4:10 states, "As every man hath received the gift, even so minister the same one to another, as good stewards of the manifold grace of God." Some people have natural talent and may not be gifted in the area of their natural talent. Some talents and gifts go together.

List some of the Spiritual Gifts in the following scriptures.

Romans 12:6-9:

_____

_____

Ephesians 4:11-12:

_____

_____

This is not a complete list of gifts.

Service: Mercy, Giving, Helps, Service
Teaching: Teaching, pastor, exhortation, evangelist
Leadership: Discerning of Spirits, faith, knowledge, leadership, pastor, teaching, wisdom, administration
Others: Apostle, Prophecy, Interpretation Tongue, Miracle, Healing

Spiritual gifts can be abused. Spiritual gifts are received and not achieved. Each member is unique with their gift. Everyone has at least one gift. Our gifts are given to help us fulfill our God given role in the Kingdom.

Discovering our Spiritual Gifts

Our gift doesn't have to be something grand; it could be as simple as being an encourager. Paul was a great encourager and that was one of his many gifts. Some of you may have the gift of being a teacher, enhance your teaching skills by proper preparation, reading, meditation on the word of God and taking classes. Remember, Spiritual Maturity is learning to obey and live a life for God.

There are some people operating in various areas of the church and it is not their gift. If you have doubt in the ministry you are serving in, you may need to re-examine why you are serving in that ministry. If you don't like what you are doing; it may not be your gift. Ministry is Free, don't require payment. If you are looking for pay, then it is not your ministry. It doesn't mean you cannot be compensated for your ministry work. It's the expectation of being compensation or the motivation of being compensated. If you only serve for money, then it's not your ministry. If money is your motivation; it's not ministry work, it a job.

When you use your gift in service, you should have a passion for it, always thinking about it and trying to improve it. Sometimes we have to encourage others to use their gift; because they may be timid, shy, or hurt by someone in the church. If someone has hurt you and you have lost your passion for service, please forgive them by letting it go. Remember, hurting people, hurt people. If we are going to stir up our gift, we must remember to use our gifts in service; second we must be good stewards of our gift. We will take a spiritual gifts survey; remember this is only a survey to help you recognize your spiritual gifts.

Spiritual Gifts Survey:

We will take a spiritual gifts survey; remember this is only a survey to help you recognize your spiritual gifts.

SPIRITUAL GIFTS SURVEY

DIRECTIONS

This is not a test, so there are no wrong answers. The *Spiritual Gifts Survey* consists of 80 statements. Select one response you feel best fit you and place that number in the blank provided. Record your answer in the blank beside each item.

- Do not spend too much time on any one item. Remember, it is not a test.

- Please give an answer for each item. Do not skip any items.

Your response choices are:

5—Highly describe me/definitely true for me

4—Most of the time this would describe me/be true for me

3—Frequently describes me/true for me about 50 percent of the time

2—Occasionally describes me/true for me about 25 percent of the time

1—Does not describe me/definitely untrue for me

_____1. I have the ability to organize ideas, resources, time, and people effectively.

_____2. I am willing to study and prepare for the task of teaching.

_____3. I am able to relate the truths of God to specific situations.

_____4. I have a God-given ability to help others grow in their faith.

_____5. I possess a special ability to communicate the truth of salvation.

_____6. I have the ability to make critical decisions when necessary.

_____7. I am sensitive to the hurts of people.

_____8. I experience joy in meeting needs through sharing possessions.

_____9. I enjoy studying.

_____10. I have delivered God's message of warning and judgment.

_____11. I am able to sense the true motivation of persons and movements.

_____12. I have a special ability to trust God in difficult situations.

_____13. I have a strong desire to contribute to the establishment of new churches.

_____14. I take action to meet physical and practical needs rather than merely talking about or planning to help.

_____15. I enjoy entertaining guests in my home.

_____16. I can adapt my guidance to fit the maturity of those working with me.

_____17. I can delegate and assign meaningful work.

_____18. I have an ability and desire to teach.

_____19. I am usually able to analyze a situation correctly.

_____20. I have a natural tendency to encourage others.

_____21. I am willing to take the initiative in helping other Christians grow in their faith.

_____22. I have an acute awareness of the emotions of other people, such as loneliness, pain, fear, and anger.

_____23. I am a cheerful giver.

_____24. I spend time digging into facts.

_____25. I feel that I have a message from God to deliver to others.

_____26. I can recognize when a person is genuine/honest.

_____27. I am a person of vision (a clear mental portrait of a preferable future given by God). I am able to communicate vision in such a way that others commit to making the vision a reality.

_____28. I am willing to yield to God's will rather than question and waver.

_____29. I would like to be more active in getting the gospel to people in other lands.

_____30. It makes me happy to do things for people in need.

_____31. I am successful in getting a group to do its work joyfully.

_____32. I am able to make strangers feel at ease.

_____33. I have the ability to plan learning approaches.

_____34. I can identify those who need encouragement.

_____35. I have trained Christians to be more obedient disciples of Christ.

_____36. I am willing to do whatever it takes to see others come to Christ.

_____37. I am attracted to people who are hurting.

_____38. I am a generous giver.

_____39. I am able to discover new truths.

_____40. I have spiritual insights from Scripture concerning issues and people that compel me to speak out.

_____41. I can sense when a person is acting in accord with God's will.

_____42. I can trust in God even when things look dark.

_____43. I can determine where God wants a group to go and help it get there.

_____44. I have a strong desire to take the gospel to places where it has never been heard.

_____45. I enjoy reaching out to new people in my church and community.

_____46. I am sensitive to the needs of people.

_____47. I have been able to make effective and efficient plans for accomplishing the goals of a group.

_____48. I often am consulted when fellow Christians are struggling to make difficult decisions.

_____49. I think about how I can comfort and encourage others in my congregation.

_____50. I am able to give spiritual direction to others.

_____51. I am able to present the gospel to lost persons in such a way that they accept the Lord and His salvation.

_____52. I possess an unusual capacity to understand the feelings of those in distress.

_____53. I have a strong sense of stewardship based on the recognition that God owns all things.

_____54. I have delivered to other persons messages that have come directly from God.

_____55. I can sense when a person is acting under God's leadership.

_____56. I try to be in God's will continually and be available for His use.

_____57. I feel that I should take the gospel to people who have different beliefs from me.

_____58. I have an acute awareness of the physical needs of others.

_____59. I am skilled in setting forth positive and precise steps of action.

_____60. I like to meet visitors at church and make them feel welcome.

_____61. I explain Scripture in such a way that others understand it.

_____62. I can usually see spiritual solutions to problems.

_____63. I welcome opportunities to help people who need comfort, consolation, encouragement, and counseling.

_____64. I feel at ease in sharing Christ with nonbelievers.

_____65. I can influence others to perform to their highest God-given potential.

_____66. I recognize the signs of stress and distress in others.

_____67. I desire to give generously and unpretentiously to worthwhile projects and ministries.

_____68. I can organize facts into meaningful relationships.

_____69. God gives me messages to deliver to His people.

_____70. I am able to sense whether people are being honest when they tell of their religious experiences.

_____71. I enjoy presenting the gospel to persons of other cultures and backgrounds.

_____72. I enjoy doing little things that help people.

_____73. I can give a clear, uncomplicated presentation.

_____74. I have been able to apply biblical truth to the specific needs of my church.

_____75. God has used me to encourage others to live Christlike lives.

_____76. I have sensed the need to help other people become more effective in their ministries.

_____77. I like to talk about Jesus to those who do not know Him.

_____78. I have the ability to make strangers feel comfortable in my home.

_____79. I have a wide range of study resources and know how to secure information.

_____80. I feel assured that a situation will change for the glory of God even when the situation seems impossible.

SPIRITUAL GIFTS SURVEY (www.lifeway.com)

SCORING YOUR SURVEY

Follow these directions to figure your score for each spiritual gift.

1. Place in each box your numerical response (1-5) to the item number which is indicated below the box.

2. For each gift, add the numbers in the boxes and put the total in the TOTAL box.

	+	+	+	+	=	
LEADERSHIP	Item 6	Item 16	Item 27	Item 43	Item 65	**TOTAL**
ADMINISTRATION	Item 1	Item 17	Item 31	Item 47	Item 59	**TOTAL**
TEACHING	Item 2	Item 18	Item 33	Item 61	Item 73	**TOTAL**
KNOWLEDGE	Item 9	Item 24	Item 39	Item 68	Item 79	**TOTAL**
WISDOM	Item 3	Item 19	Item 48	Item 62	Item 74	**TOTAL**
PROPHECY	Item 10	Item 25	Item 40	Item 54	Item 69	**TOTAL**
DISCERNMENT	Item 11	Item 26	Item 41	Item 55	Item 70	**TOTAL**
EXHORTATION	Item 20	Item 34	Item 49	Item 63	Item 75	**TOTAL**
SHEPHERDING	Item 4	Item 21	Item 35	Item 50	Item 76	**TOTAL**
FAITH	Item 12	Item 28	Item 42	Item 56	Item 80	**TOTAL**
EVANGELISM	Item 5	Item 36	Item 51	Item 64	Item 77	**TOTAL**
APOSTLESHIP	Item 13	Item 29	Item 44	Item 57	Item 71	**TOTAL**
SERVICE/HELPS	Item 14	Item 30	Item 46	Item 58	Item 72	**TOTAL**
MERCY	Item 7	Item 22	Item 37	Item 52	Item 66	**TOTAL**
GIVING	Item 8	Item 23	Item 38	Item 53	Item 67	**TOTAL**
HOSPITALITY	Item 15	Item 32	Item 45	Item 60	Item 78	**TOTAL**

Discovering Your Spiritual Gifts!

A spiritual gift is an expression of the Holy Spirit in the life of believers which empowers them to serve the body of Christ, the church. Romans 12:6-8; 1 Corinthians 12:8-10, 28-30; Ephesians 4:11; and 1 Peter 4:9-11 contain representative lists of gifts and roles God has given to the church. A definition of these gifts follows.

• **Leadership**—Leadership aids the body by leading and directing members to accomplish the goals and purposes of the church. Leadership motivates people to work together in unity toward common goals (Rom. 12:8).

• **Administration**—Persons with the gift of administration lead the body by steering others to remain on task. Administration enables the body to organize according to God-given purposes and long-term goals (1 Cor. 12:28).

• **Teaching**—Teaching is instructing members in the truths and doctrines of God's Word for the purposes of building up, unifying, and maturing the body (1 Cor. 12:28; Rom. 12:7; Eph. 4:11).

• **Knowledge**—The gift of knowledge manifests itself in teaching and training in discipleship. It is the God-given ability to learn, know, and explain the precious truths of God's Word. A word of knowledge is a Spirit-revealed truth (1 Cor. 12:28).

• **Wisdom**—Wisdom is the gift that discerns the work of the Holy Spirit in the body and applies His teachings and actions to the needs of the body (1 Cor. 12:28).

• **Prophecy**—The gift of prophecy is proclaiming the Word of God boldly. This builds up the body and leads to conviction of sin. Prophecy manifests itself in preaching and teaching (1Cor. 12:10; Rom. 12:6).

• **Discernment**—Discernment aids the body by recognizing the true intentions of those within or related to the body. Discernment tests the message and actions of others for the protection and well-being of the body (1 Cor. 12:10).

• **Exhortation**—Possessors of this gift encourage members to be involved in and enthusiastic about the work of the Lord. Members with this gift are good counselors and motivate others to service. Exhortation exhibits itself in preaching, teaching, and ministry (Rom. 12:8).

• **Shepherding**—The gift of shepherding is manifested in persons who look out for the spiritual welfare of others. Although pastors, like shepherds, do care for members of the church, this gift is not limited to a pastor or staff member (Eph. 4:11).

• **Faith**—Faith trusts God to work beyond the human capabilities of the people. Believers with this gift encourage others to trust in God in the face of apparently insurmountable odds (1 Cor. 12:9).

• **Evangelism**—God gifts his church with evangelists to lead others to Christ effectively and enthusiastically. This gift builds up the body by adding new members to its fellowship (Eph. 4:11).

• **Apostleship**—The church sends apostles from the body to plant churches or be missionaries. Apostles motivate the body to look beyond its walls in order to carry out the Great Commission (1 Cor. 12:28; Eph. 4:11).

• **Service/Helps**—Gift of service/help recognize practical needs in the body and joyfully give assistance to meeting those needs. Christians with this gift do not mind working behind the scenes (1 Cor. 12:28; Rom. 12:7).

• **Mercy**—Cheerful acts of compassion characterize those with the gift of mercy. Persons with this gift aid the body by empathizing with hurting members. They keep the body healthy and unified by keeping others aware of the needs within the church (Rom. 12:8).

• **Giving**—Members with the gift of giving give freely and joyfully to the work and mission of the body. Cheerfulness and liberality are characteristics of individuals with this gift (Rom. 12:8).

• **Hospitality**—Gift have the ability to make visitors, guests, and strangers feel at ease. They often use their home to entertain guests. Persons with this gift integrate new members into the body (1 Pet. 4:9). God has gifted you with an expression of His Holy Spirit to support His vision and mission of the church. It is a worldwide vision to reach all people with the gospel of Christ. As a servant leader, God desires that you know how He has gifted you. This will lead you to where He would have you serve as part of His vision and mission for the church.

About the Author

Thelma Alexander Bess was born and raised in Rayville, Louisiana. She is married to Rev. Lynn Bess and is the mother of two children, Chantea and Perry Jr. She has five grandchildren (Kiana, Esreal, Perry III, Macaiah & Braylon). She is the President Emeritus of the Ripley Missionary Society Convention, Former Vice President at Large of the Northeast Mississippi Baptist State Convention, Inc., Woman's Auxiliary, and the former President of the Missionary Auxiliary, Booneville Baptist Association.

She is a certified teacher by the Sunday School Publishing Board in Introduction to Leadership, Evangelism, Survey of the Book of Ruth, and History of Christianity. She is a graduate of the Dean's and President's Class in the National Congress. She enjoys public speaking and teaching. She is a Willing Worker!